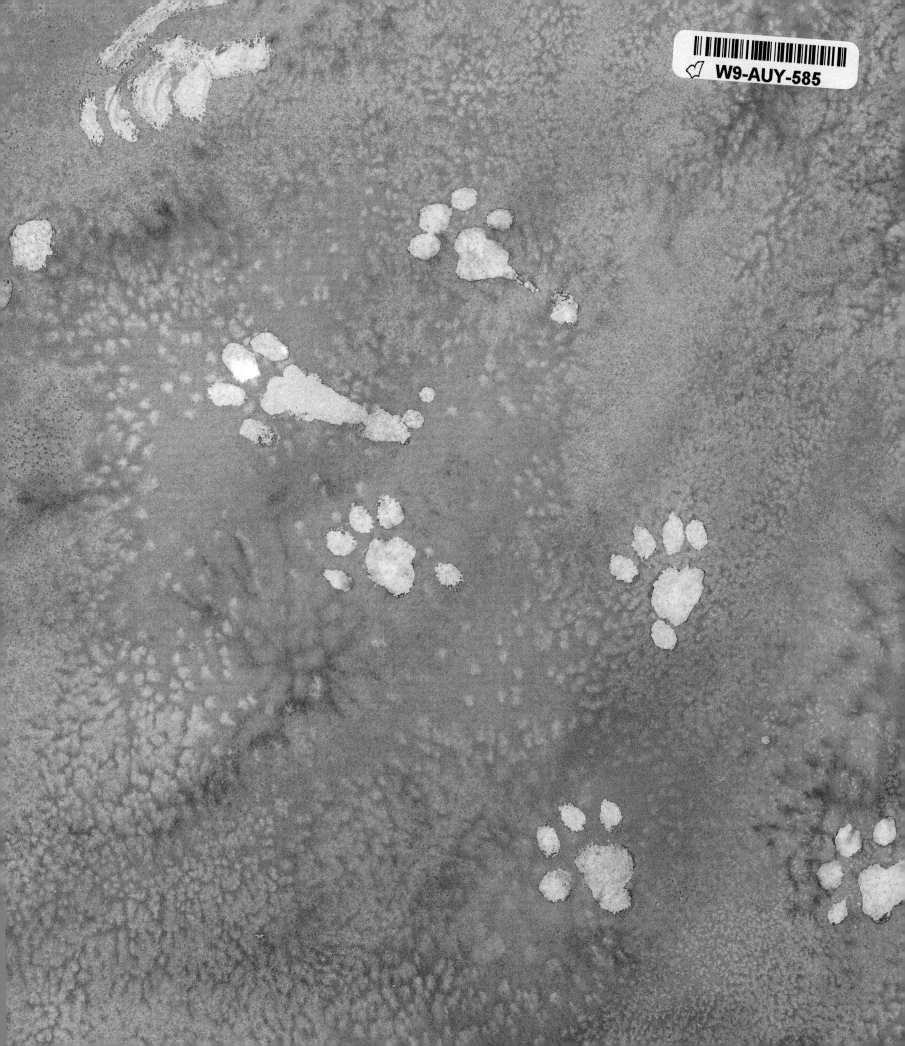

CAT!

By Virginia Kroll
Illustrated by K. Dyble Thompson

Dawn Publications

Dedication

In memory of Oakley and Annie, king and queen of all cats, and of Sugarplum and Magnolia, our little white wonders. — VK

To Michael, who knows how to pick out a cat. — KDT

A Sharing Nature With Children Book

Library of Congress Cataloging-in-Publication Data

Kroll, Virginia L.
    Cat! / by Virginia Kroll ; illustrated by K. Dyble Thompson. – 1st ed.
    p. cm. – (A Sharing nature with children book)
    Summary: Presents the characteristics and behavior of cats and describes individual breeds, including larger wild cats.
    ISBN: 1-883220-95-5 (case)
    ISBN: 1-883220-84-X (pbk.)

    1. Cats—Juvenile literature. [1. Cats.] I. Thompson, Kathryn Dyble, ill. II. Title. III Series.
SF445.7.K76 1999   636.8—dc21
                                         99-12164 CIP

Dawn Publications
P.O. Box 2010
Nevada City, CA 95959
800-545-7475
Email: nature@DawnPub.com
Website: www.DawnPub.com

Printed in Hong Kong

10 9 8 7 6 5 4 3 2 1
First Edition

Computer production by Rob Froelick

These are the cats that share a home with the author,
or with the illustrator, and helped to inspire this book:

April (by the plant)—keen and aware with her tail in the air; **Leo** (on the couch arm)—talking, pawing "people" pet; **Splotch**, (on top)—calico queen of the couch; **Panther** (right top)—inky, sleek and slinky; **Goliath** (left on couch seat)—big bold and blue; **Pearl** (center)—cute clever cream-colored kitten; **Magnus** (right on couch seat)—hefty blue-eyed and brightest white; **Zephyr** (left on floor)— purry, perky and playful; **Netty** (center, with paint brush)—the wonder cat, I wonder what she's up to? **White Sox** (right in front of couch)—cuddliest most contented creature; and **Luna** (to right of couch)—elegant and elusive.

Some popular breeds of jet black cats include the Bombay, British Black Shorthair, and Black Persian. Snow-coated cats include the White and Chinchilla Persians and the British White Shorthair.

Tortoiseshell cats have a mosaic type coat of mixed red and black.

The breeds with bluish-grey fur are Nebelung, Russian Blue, Korat, Chartreux, American Blue Burmese and the European Blue Burmese.

Calicos are white with large splotches of orange and black.

A tom is a male, and a queen is a female, especially if neither is neutered.

Coat color is often sex-linked. Tortoiseshells and calicos are almost, if not always, female. Toms are often red.

There are jet cats and snow-coated,
Torties and blues,
Tabbies and spotted,
And those of gold hues.
There are queens that are calico,
Toms that are red,
But none like the fluffy cat
Gracing my bed.

Scientists are not sure exactly how cats make the vibrating sound that we know as purring. Often, though not always, it is a sign of contentment. The jaguar, a lone hunter of Central and South American rainforests, is the only cat that does not purr.

The cheetah of Africa is the fastest land animal, reaching speeds of up to 70 miles per hour for short distances.

A new breed of cat, recognized in 1995, is the Munchkin, with short, or dwarfed, legs. Munchkins are descended from a cat found in Louisiana in the 1980s.

There are mewing cats, purring cats,
Kittens that bawl,
And cats in the wild
That don't purr at all.
There are pacing cats, racing cats,
Short cats and tall,
But none like the sleek cat
That streaks down my hall.

Many domestic cats paw with a light tap to get attention. Cats instinctively put out their claws to defend themselves. They are fond of sharpening them on scratching posts (or furniture) and, in the wild, marking territory by leaving scratch marks on trees. Cats' claws can be pulled back into their coverings, or sheaths, when not in use. The only cat with non-retractable claws is the cheetah.

Cats with extra toes are called polydactylous cats. This is the result of a mutation.

A cat sleeps more than any other animal, an average of 16 hours a day. Their sleep patterns are controlled by a chemical called melatonin that is released in their brains. They are most awake at dawn and dusk and dream as humans do.

There are pawing cats, clawing cats,
Kittens that scratch,
Cats that are kickers
With toes that don't match.
There are long dreamy snoozers
And cats that short-nap,
But none like the sleepy cat
Curled in my lap.

Staring, stalking, crouching and pouncing are all instinctive responses. A cat ready to fight or attack its prey will stare. Cats crouch low when they are fearful or when staying out of view. Because of these instincts, even well-fed indoor cats should be given toys to "hunt."

The best jumpers in the cat kingdom are the lynx of Europe and the caracal of Africa. But all cats' bodies are well-equipped to propel them forward and to take the landing force. A cat can leap three times its body length. Cats are famous for the "righting reflex" that enables a falling cat to turn in mid-air and land properly.

There are daring cats, staring cats,
Kittens that bounce,
And stealthy cats tensing
And ready to pounce.
There are leaping cats, creeping cats,
Cats in a crouch.
But none like the lolling cat
Draped on my couch.

Cats are famous for hanging around dairy barns at milking time, or greeting fishermen at the dock. Most cats like milk, although some cannot digest it well. Most cats like fish, but it is important for them to eat meat since they are carnivores.

Cats' tongues are covered with prickly, back-facing bumps called papillae, which give them their rough surface. Cats use their tongues for grooming and, in the wild, for scraping meat clean of fur and feathers, and bones clean of meat.

There are cats that like tuna
And those that love milk,
And cats with rough tongues
Of a sandpaper ilk.
There are cats that walk slowly
And cats on the run,
But none like my basking cat
Stretched in the sun.

Cats typically have one of three eye shapes: round, almond, or slanted. Gold and yellow are the eye colors most closely related to those of wild cats. If a cat has two eyes that are different colors, it is said to be "odd-eyed." Blue-eyed white cats are often deaf.

Cats can see very well in the dark. They have vertical pupils. The pupils can shrink into slits, blocking out light when needed, yet allowing light to get through when cats close their eyelids half-way. (Because lions hunt by day, they have round contracting pupils like humans do.)

Manx and Cymric cats have no tails. American Bobtail, Japanese Bobtail, and Kurile Island Bobtail cats have short, stubby tails, as do Pixiebobs. Tails of long-haired breeds are full, long, and fluffy.

There are blue-eyed cats, gold-eyed cats,
Odd-eyed and green,
With round eyes or oval
Or shaped in between,
With no tails or stub tails
Or long tails that swish—
But none like my cat
Dashing straight for its dish.

Many people wrongly believe that cats are moody, unsociable creatures. They can seem uncooperative if you try to play with them during the day, for they are by nature nocturnal animals, active mostly at night.

Some cats appear to smile, and much art and sculpture, both ancient and modern, reflect this trait. The Nebelung, a silver-tipped American blue, related to the Russian Blue, is a long hair that is recognized by its smile.

Some cats, like the Jaguar, are lone hunters and prefer a solitary life. Others, like lions, are very sociable and live in groups called prides. Generally cats like being around and near one another, especially when food is abundant. They form hierarchies according to status.

There are moody cats, broody cats,
Cats that beguile,
And cats that sit back
With a curious smile.
There are cats that pretend
To like living alone,
But none like my cat
With a mind of its own.

All cats make different sounds for different reasons. They include meows, purrs, wails, screeches, and high-intensity sounds. Male lions are famous for their loud roaring. Oriental breeds tend to be the most vocal.

The Balinese is a long-haired cousin to the Siamese. Both cats are blue-eyed and vocal. Their pale coats have points—darker color at the extremities (ears, feet, noses and tails).

Scottish Fold cats have round ears that are flattened, giving their heads a ball-shaped look.

Rexes are cats with long slender legs, dainty paws, and curly silky fur that has no guard hairs, (coarse longer hairs that protect the underfur).

There are yowling cats, howling cats,
Cats on the prowl,
And cats that can roar
With a thunderous growl.
There are Siamese, Balinese,
Fold, Rex, and more,
But none like the one
That meows at my door.

Male cats, whether neutered or not, tend to be larger than females. Most cats weigh between 5 and 15 pounds.

Though most experts agree that cats can use both paws equally well, some research indicates that most cats seem to prefer their left paws.

It is said that a dog sleeps with one eye open. By comparison, a cat could be said to sleep with both ears open. A cat's hearing is acute, three times sharper than a dog's and five times greater than a human's. A cat's ears can rotate 180 degrees, catching sounds from all angles without a move of the head.

A cat's awareness is enhanced by its whiskers. Called vibrissae or tactile hairs, they are delicate organs that help a cat to "see" by judging distance and identifying objects in the dark. A cat has about 30 whiskers, located above the eyes, on the chin, and at the sides of the mouth.

"Top cats," those that are leaders or seem to be in charge, often strut with their heads and tails held high.

There are hefty cats, lefty cats,
Keen and aware,
And cats—tails up—
With the haughtiest air.
There are cozy cats, nosy cats,
Kittens that snore,
But none like my whiz
That seems able to soar.

The ways in which cats wag their tails are clues to how they're feeling. A tail gently swishing from side to side denotes contentment. A tail jerking back and forth means concentration. A tail that is lashing hard is indicative of anger or annoyance.

Cats can brake by using the "carpal pad," a cushion found at mid-leg, that stops them from skidding. This comes in handy when a cat suddenly races around a room, sometimes at speeds greater than 30 miles per hour, as if startled. Some experts say that this is a release of a house cat's pent-up energy that it cannot expend as it could if it were wild.

Cats communicate by using body signals and scents as well as sounds. Many cats solve potential battles with certain growls, body stance, or even eye contact alone.

Cats get temporarily stuck in trees because their claws are designed for climbing up. A cat will cling until it eventually figures out how to ease its way down backwards.

Some indoor cats get so excited when watching prey, such as birds, that their teeth will actually chatter, or they will let out a kind of quick rhythmic chortle.

There are wagging cats, tagging cats,
Ready to clash.
There are clinging cats, zinging cats,
On a mad dash.
There are cats that communicate
Well without words,
But none like my window cat
Watching the birds.

All over the world, the magical, mystical, clever cat has given rise to folklore, fairy tales, legends, poems, plays, proverbs and cartoons. Cat totems, or symbolic animals, are associated with the qualities of mystery, magic, and independence.

Cats are considered the spiritual bridges from human beings to other animals. They are thought to be close to the spirit world in general. It was believed that witches used cats as their familiars, or companion animals, because they were spirits in disguise.

A cat's stately pose and grand demeanor suggest a sense of being steady and untouched by any circumstance. Many people admire the cat for its self-reliant streak and ability to fend for itself.

Many cats show affection to their owners only in their own way, but some readily come when they are beckoned.

There are stay-home, contented cats,
Cats on the go,
And cats that see worlds
That we humans don't know.
There are cats that seem bothered
By nothing at all,
But none like this creature
That comes when I call.

Most cats, especially when young, are very inquisitive and love to explore.

Scruffing is the way a mother cat transports her kittens. She carries them in her mouth by the backs, or scruffs, of their necks. During scruffing, a cat instinctively stops moving and brings its legs close to its body to prevent injury. This response stays with a cat throughout its life.

Some long-haired cat breeds are Turkish Van, Turkish Angora, Maine Coon, Norwegian Forest, Persian, and Somali.

Short-haired cats are easily groomed, and include Exotic short-hair, Abyssinian, Burmese, Singapura, Tonkinese, Burmilla, American Shorthair and British Shorthair.

Some breeds have curly hair and whiskers, such as La Perm and Rex. American Wirehair Cats' coats are of medium length and are tightly crimped and springy.

Certain breeds, like Egyptian Mau, Siamese, Oriental Short-hair, and Havana, have long, narrow faces.

26

There are curious kittens
And those that are scruffed;
Short-haired or long-haired
Or curly or fluffed;
Cats with slim faces
Or heads nearly round,
But none like the beauty
I picked from the pound.

Cats, nearly always clean and quiet, are ideal pets for apartment dwellers.

Unfortunately, some feral, or wild, cats must forage in garbage dumps and seek their own shelter wherever they find a dry place. Help comes from caring people, the SPCA, and pounds.

Many farmers appreciate barn cats, who keep down the rodent population in silos and stalls where grains and other feed are stored.

Cats figure into early Christian art, especially with the Virgin Mary, and are associated with many saints, including St. Jerome, St. Agatha, St. Gertrude of Nivelles, and St. Francis of Assisi.

In Islam, cats are allowed to roam freely in mosques because of legends about them and Mohammed.

Cats are kept as mousers in Buddhist temples throughout Asia. People of the Hindu and Parsee religions have great reverence for cats. Peruvian people worshipped a puma god, and many Egyptians had a cat god called Bastet.

Contrary to popular belief, all cats do not hate water. The serval never strays far from it in its southern African habitat. The bobcat of North America is fond of swamps. The tiger of Asia frequently finds a lake to cool off in. The Fishing Cat of Asia has slightly webbed feet.

There are city cats, gritty cats,
Barn cats in stalls,
Cats in cathedrals
And in temple walls.
There are shore cats, indoor cats,
And cats on the roam,
But none like the cat
Making my house a home.

Some cats, like the Oriental Short-hair, are particularly sleek and graceful in appearance.

 The black panther, previously thought to be a separate species of wild cat, is actually a dark variety of leopard. People have deliberately bred domestic cats to have this variation in coat color. The Bombay was the first cat bred to look like a miniature panther.

The Sphynx, a big-eared cat, appears to be hairless, but is actually covered with fine down.

Distinctive ear tufts are found on some wild cats, such as the lynx and caracal.

There are slinky cats, inky cats,
Cats with no hair,
And cats with a tuft
On the tip of each ear.
There are spunky cats, clever,
Courageous, and smart,
But none like the one cat
That's captured my heart!

Virginia Kroll does not do her writing in a secluded cabin or an ivory tower, but in her own home that bustles with the activities of her six children and many other members of the household—including nine cats. She lives life intensely, feeling both the joys and pains of everyone. She is also a prolific writer, at least in the very early hours of the morning when everyone else is asleep. The strength of her compassion and perception come through in her other books published by Dawn Publications: *Motherlove, With Love to Earth's Endangered Peoples* and *When God Made the Tree*.

K. Dyble Thompson's nickname is Kitty, which along with her professional accomplishments, gives her unique qualifications to illustrate this book. Kitty's cat is named Netty, who showed an unusual degree of interest in this project. "Netty" is a short for Bayonet, which is a commentary on his claws. Kitty has a degree in fine arts from the University of Wisconsin at Milwaukee. In addition to her book illustrations, she is known as a muralist and a pavement artist. She also illustrated *When Brian Hugged His Mother* for Dawn Publications.

ALSO BY VIRGINIA KROLL

Motherlove. The love of a mother for her young, it is said, is the closest echo of love divine. This book is a celebration of motherlove—in both animals and humans.

With Love, to Earth's Endangered Peoples. All over the world, groups of people are in danger of losing their age-old ways forever. Often they have a beautiful, meaningful relationship with Earth. This book portrays several of them, with love.

When God Made the Tree. Children and creatures all over the world depend on trees for food, shelter and comfort. People, animals and trees are forever linked in an intimate relationship that suggests the greatness of their Creator.

OTHER DISTINCTIVE NATURE AWARENESS BOOKS FROM DAWN PUBLICATIONS

Stickeen: John Muir and the Brave Little Dog, by John Muir as retold by Donnell Rubay. John Muir's favorite story of "the most memorable of all my wild days"—his classic adventure on an Alaskan glacier with the dog Stickeen—is now retold in modern language with stunning illustrations. Winner of the Benjamin Franklin Award for "Best Nature Book."

The Dandelion Seed, by Joseph Anthony. The humble dandelion. By roadside or mountainside, it flowers every month of the year throughout the world, a fitting symbol of life. Its journey is our journey, filled with challenge, wonder and beauty. Winner of the Benjamin Franklin Silver Award for "Best Children's Picture Book."

This is the Sea that Feeds Us, by Robert F. Baldwin. This book links a fish dinner enjoyed by a thankful family with the entire marine food web. Each verse introduces a new link and then connects it to everything else. Recipient of the "Teacher's Choice" Award by the International Reading Association.

Dawn Publications is dedicated to inspiring in children a deeper understanding and appreciation for all life on Earth. To order, or for a copy of our catalog, please call 800-545-7475. Please also visit our web site at www.DawnPub.com.

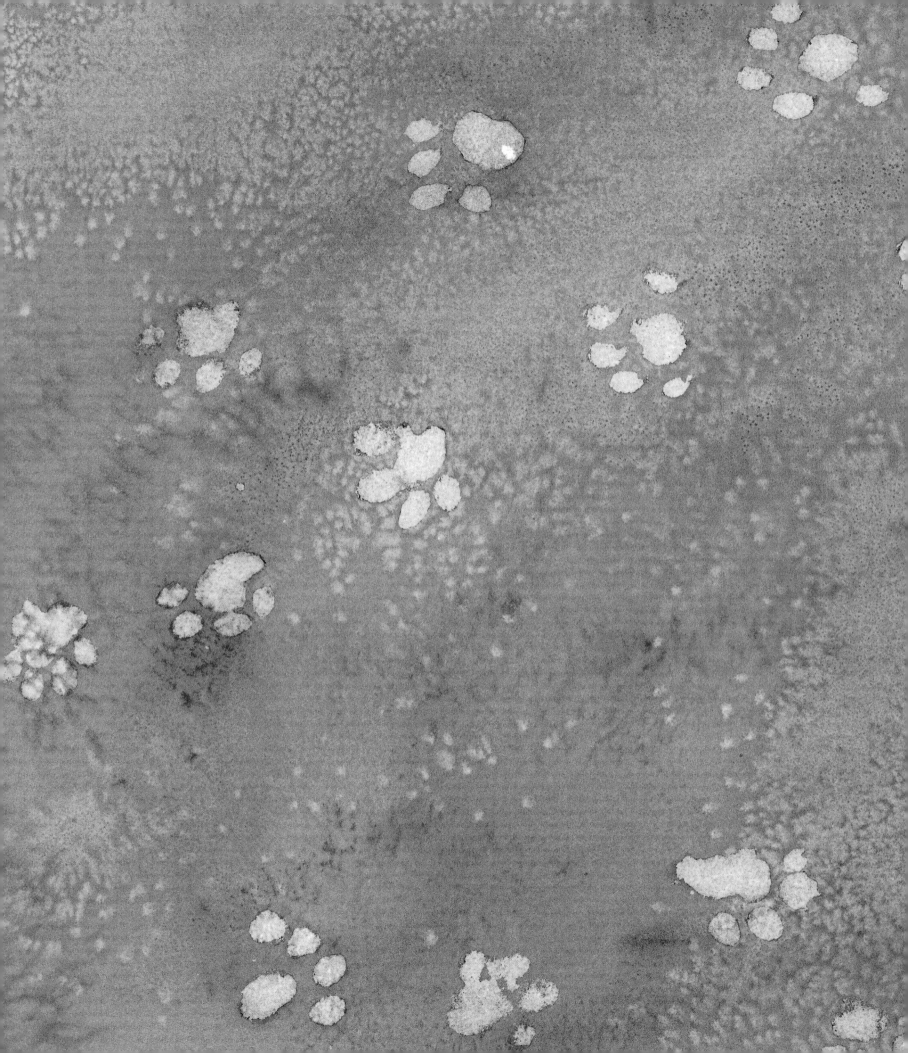